XHOSA

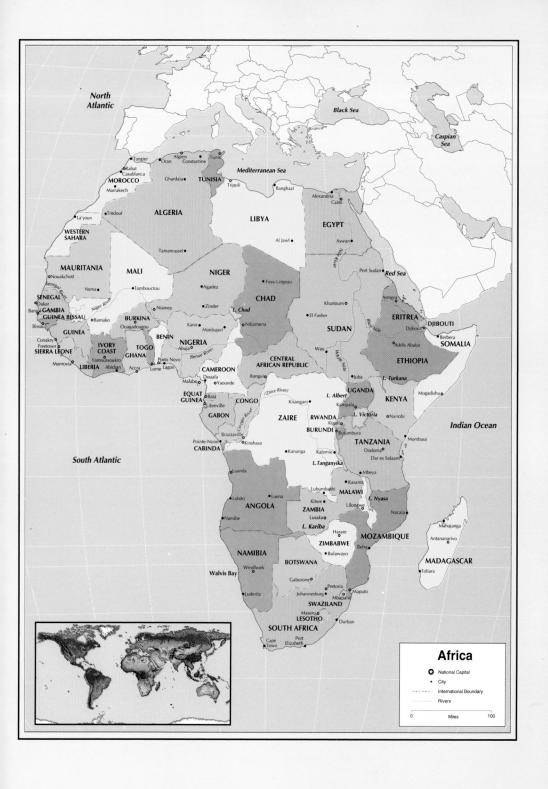

North
Atlantic

Black Sea

Caspian
Sea

Tangier
Rabat
Casablanca
MOROCCO
Marrakech
Ghardaia
Oran
Algiers
Constantine
Tunis
TUNISIA

Mediterranean Sea

Tripoli
Banghazi
Alexandria
Cairo

La'youn
Tindouf
WESTERN
SAHARA

ALGERIA

LIBYA

EGYPT

Aswan

Al Jawf

MAURITANIA
Nouakchott
Nema

MALI

NIGER

CHAD

Port Sudan
Red Sea

Agadez
Faya-Largeau

Tamanrasset

Asmera
ERITREA

Senegal River
SENEGAL
Dakar
GAMBIA
Banjul
GUINEA BISSAU
Bissau
GUINEA
Conakry
Freetown
SIERRA LEONE
Monrovia
LIBERIA

Tombouctou
Niger River
Niamey
Zinder
Bamako
Ouagadougou
BURKINA
Kano
Maiduguri
BENIN
NIGERIA
Abuja
Benue River
TOGO
GHANA
Porto Novo
Lome
Lagos
Accra
Abidjan
Yamoussoukro
IVORY
COAST

L. Chad
Ndjamena

Zinder

El Fasher
Khartoum

SUDAN

Blue Nile

Djibouti
DJIBOUTI
Addis Ababa
Berbera
SOMALIA

Wau
White Nile

CENTRAL
AFRICAN REPUBLIC

Bangui

Juba

ETHIOPIA

L. Turkana

Mogadishu

CAMEROON
Douala
Yaounde
Malabo
EQUAT.
GUINEA
Bata
Libreville
GABON
CONGO

(Zaire River)

Kisangani

L. Albert
UGANDA
Kampala
L. Victoria

KENYA

Nairobi

Brazzaville
Pointe-Noire
Kinshasa
CABINDA

CONGO River

ZAIRE

Kananga

RWANDA
Kigali
BURUNDI
Bujumbura

TANZANIA
Dodoma
Dar es Salaam

Mombasa

Indian Ocean

South Atlantic

Luanda

Kalemie

L. Tanganyika

Mbeya

Lobito
Luena
ANGOLA
Namibe

Lubumbashi
Kitwe
ZAMBIA
Lusaka
L. Kariba

Kasama
MALAWI
Lilongwe
L. Nyasa

Nacala

Mahajanga

Antananarivo

NAMIBIA
Walvis Bay
Windhoek
Luderitz

BOTSWANA
Gaborone

Harare
ZIMBABWE
Bulawayo
MOZAMBIQUE
Beira

MADAGASCAR

Toliara

Pretoria
Johannesburg
Maputo
Mbabane
SWAZILAND
Maseru
LESOTHO
Durban
SOUTH AFRICA
Cape
Town
Port
Elizabeth

Africa

✪ National Capital
• City
- - - - International Boundary
—— Rivers

0   Miles   100

The Heritage Library of African Peoples

XHOSA

Russell Kaschula, Ph.D.

THE ROSEN PUBLISHING GROUP, INC.
NEW YORK

Published in 1997 by The Rosen Publishing Group, Inc.
29 East 21st Street, New York, NY 10010

First Edition

Manufactured in the United States of America

Library of Congress Cataloging-in-Publication Data

Kaschula, Russell.
    Xhosa/Russell Kaschula.—1st ed.
        p.   cm.—(The heritage library of African peoples)
    Includes bibliographical references and index.
    Summary: Surveys the culture, history, and contemporary life of
the Xhosa people of South Africa.
    ISBN 0-8239-2013-5
    1. Xhosa (African people)—History—Juvenile literature.
2. Xhosa (African people)—Social life and customs—Juvenile
literature.   I. Title.   II. Series.
DT1768.X57K37   1997
968′.004963985—dc20   96-42271
                                                        CIP
                                                        AC

Contents

INTRODUCTION

THERE IS EVERY REASON FOR US TO KNOW something about Africa and to understand its past and the way of life of its peoples. Africa is a rich continent that has for centuries provided the world with art, culture, labor, wealth, and natural resources. It has vast mineral deposits, fossil fuels, and commercial crops.

But perhaps most important is the fact that fossil evidence indicates that human beings originated in Africa. The earliest traces of human beings and their tools are almost two million years old. Their descendants have migrated throughout the world. To be human is to be of African descent.

The experiences of the peoples who stayed in Africa are as rich and as diverse as of those who established themselves elsewhere. This series of books describes their environment, their modes of subsistence, their relationships, and their customs and beliefs. The books present the variety of languages, histories, cultures, and religions that are to be found on the African continent. They demonstrate the historical linkages between African peoples and the way contemporary Africa has been affected by European colonial rule.

Africa is large, complex, and diverse. It encompasses an area of more than 11,700,000

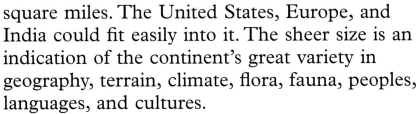

square miles. The United States, Europe, and India could fit easily into it. The sheer size is an indication of the continent's great variety in geography, terrain, climate, flora, fauna, peoples, languages, and cultures.

Much of contemporary Africa has been shaped by European colonial rule, industrialization, urbanization, and the demands of a world economic system. For more than seventy years, large regions of Africa were ruled by Great Britain, France, Belgium, Portugal, and Spain. African peoples from various ethnic, linguistic, and cultural backgrounds were brought together to form colonial states.

For decades Africans struggled to gain their independence. It was not until after World War II that the colonial territories became independent African states. Today, almost all of Africa is ruled by Africans. Large numbers of Africans live in modern cities. Rural Africa is also being transformed, and yet its people still engage in many of their customs and beliefs.

Contemporary circumstances and natural events have not always been kind to ordinary Africans. Today, however, new popular social movements and technological innovations pose great promise for future development.

George C. Bond, Ph.D., Director
Institute of African Studies
Columbia University, New York

The Xhosa language is spoken by over 7 million South Africans, making Xhosa speakers one of the country's most important groups. They are also well known for the beautiful beadwork they often wear on special occasions. This photograph, taken in the 1960s, shows two young men wearing their finest outfits.

chapter

1

EMAXHOSENI—"THE PLACE WHERE THE XHOSA LIVE"

IN SOUTH AFRICA, THE XHOSA-SPEAKING people form the second largest language group. The Xhosa language, which features many click sounds, is spoken by almost 7 million people— roughly 18 percent of the South African population.

The Xhosa people as a whole consist of many different chiefdoms. They are named after a heroic ancestor from the distant past called Xhosa. Only two of the oldest chiefdoms, the Gcaleka and Rharhabe, can claim direct descent from him. They are sometimes called the "Xhosa proper," to set them apart from the many other Xhosa speakers.

Other major Xhosa-speaking chiefdoms are the Thembu, Bomvana, Mpondo, and Mpondomise. Xhosa speakers who are less closely related include the Mfengu, who fled into Xhosa territory from the north in the 1800s, and the Bhaca, Bhele, Zizi, Hlubi, and

LANGUAGE

Xhosa contains click sounds borrowed from Khoisan languages. Khoisan peoples, including both Khoekhoe and San (Bushman) peoples, were among the earliest inhabitants of southern Africa. Their language and culture have had a strong influence on many peoples in the region.

Three basic clicks are used when speaking Xhosa. The first is "c" (front click), as in *icici* (an earring). This click is produced by placing the tip of your tongue behind your upper front teeth and then suddenly pulling the tongue downward. The lips should be formed into a smile but only slightly parted.

The second click is "q" (top click), as in *iqaqa* (skunk). The tongue is placed against the middle of the roof of your mouth and then quickly moved downward. Here the lips keep an O shape and the mouth is opened while producing the sound.

The third click is "x" (side click), as in *uxam* (water lizard). The tip of the tongue is placed on the front part of the roof of the mouth. The tongue is pulled downward and backward, allowing air to escape on both sides of the tongue.

These basic clicks, used in combination with certain consonants, create other types of clicks. For example, *ingca* (grass) uses "c" and "ng" to form the "ngc" click, and *igqirha* (doctor) uses the "gq" click. The name "Xhosa" is similar, but those who have not learned the click pronounce the word "caw-suh" or "haw-suh."

Xhosa is a tonal language. Thus, the word *uyagula* can have two completely different meanings depending on how it is pronounced. If the second to last syllable is lengthened, then it is a statement: "He or she is ill." But if the tone rises at the end, then it is a question: "Is he or she ill?"

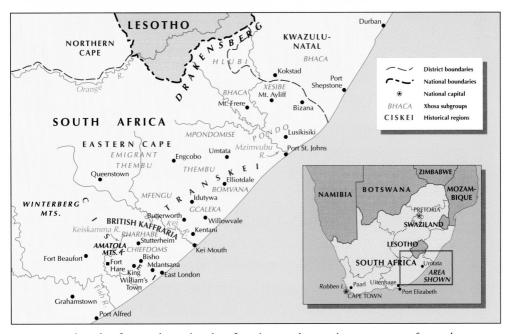

Today the former homelands of Ciskei and Transkei are part of South Africa's Eastern Cape province. The regions associated with the various Xhosa-speaking subgroups are also marked.

Qwati. They all live mainly in the Eastern Cape, although they are found throughout South Africa.

Each of these chiefdoms speaks a slightly different dialect, or variation, of Xhosa, but they can all understand each other. The first Xhosa dialect to be written down was recorded among the people of Chief Ngqika of the Rharhabe. This became standard Xhosa.

Each Xhosa chiefdom consists of a number of clans. Each clan is composed of people related to the same male ancestor. Clan members do not marry each other, since they are related.

During the 1600s and 1700s, the Xhosa-speaking people settled on the mountain slopes of the Amatola and the Winterberg Mountains. The many streams in the region drain into the

11

great rivers of Xhosa territory, including the Kei River and the Fish River. Rich soils and plentiful rainfall make the river basins good for farming and grazing.

Starting in the late 1700s, British authorities and British and Dutch settlers began to take over much of Xhosa territory. For a hundred years, Xhosa speakers resisted fiercely. Nine frontier wars were fought. By the end of the 1800s Xhosa speakers lost much of their territory to the British who were then trying to take control of South Africa.

▼ MODERN SOUTH AFRICA ▼

In 1910 the Union of South Africa was formed. It joined together the parts of South Africa that had been under the separate control of the British and Dutch settlers.

From 1948 until 1994, South Africa was ruled by the Nationalist Party, a group composed largely of Afrikaners. The Afrikaners are descendants of early Dutch settlers in southern Africa. The Nationalist government created apartheid, a system that kept ethnic groups and races apart.

Under apartheid, 87 percent of the territory of South Africa was reserved for whites, who made up only 13 percent of the population. Blacks had few rights in these white areas. They were forced to live in ethnic reserves called "homelands." The name homelands was misleading because the

During the apartheid era blacks were forced to live in ethnic reserves called homelands. Seen here is a village in the former homeland of Transkei.

reserves contained only a small amount of the territory that had belonged to these peoples before the whites arrived. Often, blacks were allowed to keep only the most barren and unwanted parts of their former land.

Until 1994 the Xhosa-speaking peoples lived mainly in the homelands of Transkei and Ciskei. These homelands were declared "independent" countries by the apartheid government. However, they were not recognized as independent, self-ruled nations by the United Nations. This was because the world knew that the homelands were just part of a plan by the white government to prevent blacks from having real rights in South Africa.

Blacks had to have permits to leave the home-lands to live and work in wealthier parts of South Africa. They were kept separate and forced to live in black townships, or segregated communities on the outskirts of white cities and towns in

13

NELSON MANDELA

Nelson Mandela is the most famous Xhosa leader. He was born on July 18, 1918 at Mvezo, a small village near Umtata. He comes from the royal Thembu clan of Madiba. Mandela is often called Madiba as a sign of respect.

As a young boy, Mandela moved north with his mother to the small village of Qunu. Mandela's father was a chief. After a disagreement with a local white authority, Mandela's father was punished by the loss of his position. Mandela was then reared by the Thembu royal family, the Dalindyebo family.

Mandela studied law at Fort Hare University. Later he moved to Johannesburg. There he worked in a legal firm with a friend, Walter Sisulu. The two men became leading figures in the ANC, which fought for democracy and equality for all people.

The white Nationalist Party government refused to listen to the peaceful protests of the ANC and the majority of South Africans. In 1962 the ANC formed a military wing called Umkhonto WeSizwe, meaning the Spear of the Nation, to fight for freedom. Members, including Mandela, received military training outside South Africa. In 1963 Mandela was arrested on his return to South Africa. He was convicted of treason and sentenced to life imprisonment on Robben Island. Mandela spent twenty-seven years in jail.

The struggle for freedom lasted decades. Many Xhosa people went into exile in other African countries. Others settled in Europe and America. From the 1960s onward, the black people of South Africa resisted the white Nationalist government in every possible way. Opponents of apartheid suffered terrible oppression. The world also increasingly rejected the racist regime in South Africa.

In 1990 the white Nationalist government realized that it had to negotiate with the ANC and make democratic reforms in South Africa. Mandela's release was followed by many years of careful negotiation between the numerous political groups in South Africa. Mandela and F. W. De Klerk, the Nationalist leader, guided South Africa toward free elections. With remarkably little violence, the elections concluded a revolution in South Africa. The orderly transfer of power from the white minority to the black majority drew international praise. Mandela and De Klerk both won the Nobel Peace Prize for their leadership.

President Nelson Mandela played a leading role in the struggle for democracy in South Africa. He is fondly named Madiba, after the Thembu royal clan to which he belongs.

South Africa. Many Xhosa speakers who worked in Cape Town lived in the townships of Khayelitsha, Langa, and Guguletu. Others lived in townships outside other big towns in the Eastern Cape and in Soweto near Johannesburg. Many still live in these townships today.

South Africa held its first democratic elections in 1994, and blacks were finally allowed to vote. The white Nationalist government was defeated by the African National Congress (ANC), and the apartheid and homeland systems were abolished. Nelson Mandela, a Xhosa man, was elected president in May 1994. This ended a long and often violent struggle for freedom and democracy in South Africa.▲

chapter

2

RELIGION

IN 1799 DR. JOHANNES VAN DER KEMP, A Dutch missionary belonging to the London Missionary Society, began his work among the Xhosa. Missionaries converted many Xhosa to Christianity. Those who refused to convert were called amaQaba, meaning the red people. This is because they anointed themselves with red ocher, or clay, from the earth to signify their sacred links to their ancestors. It was through their ancestors that they worshipped their own Supreme Being, Qamata. AmaQaba kept their traditions.

▼ ANCESTORS ▼

The amaQaba believed that the ancestors guarded their living relatives and communicated their prayers to Qamata. Ancestors had to be continually honored, particularly through the

Xhosa traditionalists were known as amaQaba, the red people, after the red ocher they wore and rubbed into their clothes. These amaQaba women are tending a pineapple field.

ceremonial sacrifice of cattle or goats. If they were neglected or ignored, the ancestors could cause misfortune or illness for their living family members.

Today many Xhosa people continue to revere their ancestors. Although the early missionaries fought strongly against this, many Christian churches now allow ancestor worship.

The missionaries introduced an alternative Christian name for Qamata: Thixo. Among the Xhosa this is still the most widely used name for God, but many other praise names exist, such as uDali, the Creator; uMenzi, the One who Acts; and Nkosi yoHlanga, King of the Nation.

▼ MISSIONARIES ▼

The missionaries insisted that Xhosa converts give up worshipping their ancestors. Polygyny, the practice of having more than one wife, and other customs were forbidden. Traditional clothing and houses were discouraged. Converts were expected to wear Western clothing, which they found hot and impractical, and to build neat circular cottages that the missionaries found acceptable. Many missionaries, however, wanted to protect their communities of converts against white colonials and the government. Since the missionaries spoke the Xhosa language, they could mediate between the Xhosa people and the white authorities to benefit the converts. Mission schools taught Western values to an educated elite that included many future leaders.

Missionaries discouraged many aspects of Xhosa tradition. However, they also often protected their Xhosa converts from the abuses of the white colonial government. Today many Xhosa are Christian.

AFRICANIST CHURCHES

From the 1890s on, new churches were started. They harmonized traditional African beliefs with Christianity. In particular they allowed the worship of ancestors along with the worship of God. In the African view, ancestors are simply a way of reaching God, just as in some Western churches people pray to the Christian saints. These churches became known as Africanist churches.

Today the two most important Africanist churches are the Zionist and the Ethiopian churches. The Ethiopian churches are modeled on Western churches. They have little to do with traditional African religion, besides the fact that their church officials are always black. The Zionist, or Apostolic churches, however, openly combine Christianity with elements of traditional African religion.

Today preachers from the independent churches are given airtime in order to broadcast their messages. They discuss how ancestor worship relates to Christianity. Such broadcasts are part of an ongoing exploration of Xhosa tradition, which continually finds new ways to adapt to the present.

Many Xhosa belong to traditional Western churches, such as the Anglican Church. Until 1996 the Anglican Archbishop of Cape Town was Desmond Tutu, a Xhosa speaker. His parents' family lived in the Qumbu district of Transkei.

Archbishop Tutu preached liberation theology. He argued that the church could not stand by and watch the abuses of apartheid. Rather, it needed to be actively involved in working for liberation. He received the Nobel Peace Prize in 1984 for the way he used the Christian message to promote democracy and peace in South Africa.

Desmond Tutu is now the chairperson of South Africa's Truth and Reconciliation Commission. It hears cases dealing with horrific acts committed during the apartheid era.

▼ DIVINERS ▼

Any illness among Xhosa people—physical, psychological, or spiritual—was (and often still is) treated by an *igqirha*, a traditional healer or diviner.

Xhosa people see diviners as gifted individuals who communicate directly with the ancestors through dreams. Diviners' dreams are often prophetic, predicting future events. Diviners also communicate with the ancestors through a trance-like state called *thwasa*. This powerful spiritual experience enables diviners to heal others. The practice of spiritual healing with the help of the ancestors is now part of the Africanist churches. Traditional healers have different ways of healing. For example, the *ixhwele*, or herbalist,

This woman is a diviner's assistant. She wears white beads, associated with diviners, and a special headdress. Her leg bracelets are made from intertwined roots from a tree.

The rock seen above was the favorite seat of Ndlambe, a famous Xhosa chief who used to hold meetings there. The diviner on the right is preparing to conduct a rainmaking ceremony. She holds an oryx horn, while the young man above her blows a kudu horn, an instrument like a trumpet.

uses plant medicines to treat physical illnesses. Vebal techniques are used by the *igqirha lokuvumisa*, meaning the diviner who seeks affirmation. With the guidance of the ancestors, she makes a series of statements about a problem. If she is on the right track, her clients shout out, "*Siyavuma*," meaning we agree. Together, they arrive at the cause of the problem, after which the diviner prescribes a cure. It takes at least

21

This Xhosa diviner wears a fur headdress and cape. Like most diviners, white beadwork is an important part of her outfit.

five years of apprenticeship to become a diviner.

Today many Xhosa people visit both a Western medical doctor and a traditional diviner. There is also increasing cooperation between medical doctors and diviners, as each recognizes the other's skills. It is now known that many traditional medicines made from plants are effective. Most diviners today are women.▲

chapter

3

SOCIETY AND CUSTOMS

IN THE PAST, XHOSA DAILY LIFE MOVED AT a dignified pace and with a sense that the ancestors watched over everything. Today many Xhosa people have lifestyles very similar to those of other city dwellers all over the world. It is mainly in the rural areas of South Africa that many still follow tradition, although aspects of tradition also remain important to many urban Xhosa.

▼ CATTLE ▼

Cattle play a key role in traditional Xhosa life. A rural family's wealth was, and often still is, measured by the number of cattle it owns. Cattle are the basis of the economy. They also serve to unite families. A bride-price of several cattle, called *lobola*, must be paid to the bride's family upon marriage. This payment of cattle makes the children of the marriage legitimate.

23

Cattle are the cornerstone of the traditional Xhosa family. In the past, a man had to pay several cattle to his bride's family in order to marry. Wealthy men with large herds could marry several wives. Today most men have only one wife, and cash payments often replace the payment of cattle. Seen above is a man and his two wives.

Cattle are also vital for communicating with the ancestors. They are sacrificed in honor of the ancestors at all important feasts and ceremonies. The animal is pricked with a spear until it bellows, which indicates that the ancestors approve and will bless the ceremony. Hearing the bellow, the crowd calls out, "*Camagu,*" which means much the same as amen.

Cows are milked in the corral, or kraal, every morning and evening. The milk is sometimes drunk fresh. The remaining milk is placed in gourd containers to sour. This fermented milk is known as *amasi*.

Boys in rural areas must tend their families' animals at an early age. This shepherd is grazing his flock along the Wild Coast of the former Transkei.

The male head of the family controls the cattle. This means that he also is in charge of the family finances and religious sacrifices. Male children in rural areas learn to look after cattle and other herd animals at a young age.

The area between the kraal and the several houses that make up the family homestead is the *inkundla*. This is where most social and ceremonial activities take place.

▼ WORK ▼

In traditional society, men looked after the cattle and built the permanent structures, such as houses.

HOMESTEADS

The rural Xhosa family home, or homestead, includes the corral and separate houses for the husband, each of his wives, and each adult child or relative.

The earliest Xhosa houses were beehive-shaped, with thatch attached to a timber framework. Houses were normally positioned to face the rising sun. Missionaries encouraged the building of more solid houses, called *rondavels*. These round houses had mud walls, plastered over a framework of branches, and a cone-shaped, thatched roof. Today many rural dwellings are made from bricks and cement, are rectangular in shape, and have corrugated iron roofs.

Now and in the past, the *umninimzi*, or head of the rural homestead, is the senior male of the family. He lives with his wife or wives, his unmarried children, and sometimes one or two dependent relatives. Polygyny, the practice of having more than one wife at the same time, was the ideal but not necessarily the norm; today it is increasingly rare.

Today many poor city dwellers live in rough houses made of corrugated iron, cardboard, wood, zinc, plastic, or any material that the builders can find. This is true, for example, in the sprawling township of Khayelitsha near Cape Town. Their lifestyle contrasts sharply with the wealthier urban Xhosa, many of whom now live in city apartments and suburban houses that were once reserved exclusively for whites.

Cape Town (above) has a high percentage of Xhosa people. Many of them live in poor conditions in sprawling townships and squatter camps (below).

Women farmed crops, prepared the meals, and maintained the houses. This strict division of household labor is not always the case today.

The migrant worker system changed the traditional Xhosa way of life. From the late 1800s on, rural Xhosa men began to travel far from home to earn wages in the mines, in industries, and on white-owned farms. They needed cash to pay the taxes demanded by colonial authorities. Often they were (and still are) housed in single-sex hostels. The hostels were built by the major mining groups such as the Anglo-American Corporation. In most cases migrant laborers returned to their rural homes only once or twice a year.

Rural men generally spend long periods away from home working as migrant laborers. Important ceremonies are often delayed until the men return for vacation. This man wears a long necklace of blue beads that is used when making sacrifices to the ancestors. He carries a tobacco bag.

While men were away, the remaining members of the rural Xhosa family had to bear the full responsibility of tending to the homestead, the herds, and the farms. Today many rural women act as the heads of their households. This is often due to single parenthood or because their husbands work and live in the city. The structure of the family and the roles of family members are continually changing.

▼ FOOD ▼

In the past rural Xhosa ate mainly sorghum. Today their diet consists of corn and milk. Pumpkins, beans, and other vegetables and tobacco are grown in gardens some distance from the homesteads.

Corn is eaten in many different forms. Most often it is ground into a fine meal, called mealie meal, or *umphokoqo*. Corn

Corn, which many women grind by hand, is a staple of the rural Xhosa family diet. This woman performs the task while her baby sleeps on her back.

The women at this celebration drink *umqombothi* (traditional beer) from a tin pail. Until recently, Xhosa women often smoked long pipes, such as the one seen here.

is combined with beans, pumpkins, or spinach to make a variety of traditional dishes that are still enjoyed by many South Africans. Many Western foods are also commonly eaten. People can buy meat at stores. However, they still must purchase live animals for religious sacrifices.

Umqombothi is an extremely popular traditional beer. It is offered to the ancestors at traditional ceremonies. Today it is also mass-produced in a nourishing, low-alcohol form for everyday consumption.

▼ THE CHIEF ▼

Each Xhosa chiefdom is headed by a paramount (leading) chief, or king. He is generally the eldest son of the former paramount chief and the chief's great wife. The great wife is the wife chosen by the paramount chief to be the mother of his heir; her children continue the royal line and make up the royal house. If a paramount chief dies while his heir is still too young to rule, a regent may be chosen to rule until the heir is old enough.

A chiefdom consists of several smaller territories. Each is under the authority of a lesser chief. His homestead is known as *ikomkhulu*, meaning the great place. In traditional Xhosa society, the head of each homestead acknowledged his chief by paying tribute to him. In return for the tribute paid, the chief protected those under his control and judged disputes according to traditional law. He also held all the land in trust and allotted plots to the homesteads under his authority.

In the past and in many instances today, the chief presides over all important local occasions. The Congress of Traditional Leaders of South Africa (Contralesa), an important political organization led by Chief Phatekile Holomisa, has made sure that all chiefs were represented in the new South African constitution.

Among the paramounts today are Paramount Chief Maxhoba Sandile of the Ngqika, who was installed in 1992, and Paramount Chief Buyelekhaya Dalindyebo of the Thembu, who was installed in 1993.

Chiefs continue to play an important role in Xhosa society. Seen here is the installation (crowning) ceremony of a chief. He is seated at the center of these senior men.

▼ INITIATION ▼

Over the centuries there have been numerous changes in the Xhosa way of life. Many customs are no longer followed today. However, initiation ceremonies are still important among the Xhosa-speaking groups from the western parts of the Eastern Cape. Young adults of both sexes must undergo initiation. Only then are they recognized as mature members of their communities and allowed to marry.

At about the age of eighteen, Xhosa men are circumcised in a group. In the past this ceremony took place around June. Now it normally takes place during the long Christmas holidays in December, which is midsummer in South Africa.

A few weeks before the ceremony, boys usually decorate themselves with feather headdresses and ocher paint, signifying their last days of boyhood freedom.

On the day of the ceremony, guests gather from far and wide. The men build the wood frame of the circumcision hut, or *ibhuma*, in a secluded area. Women thatch it with grass. The initiates are led to the hut by a group of skillful stick fighters. Stick fighting is a national sport among Xhosa men. The stick in the left hand is used to stop the opponent's attack. The stick in the right hand is used for hitting. It

Men's initiation is one Xhosa tradition that is still strictly followed, even in urban areas. This boy's white chalk and feather headdress indicate that he is in the first stage of initiation.

After circumcision, initiates spend several weeks in an isolated hut, where they are instructed in Xhosa customs and rules of respect. A young assistant (right) visits the parents of each initiate to fetch the meals they each prepare for their sons.

can be a dangerous game, and the sight of blood is not uncommon.

An animal sacrifice is made, and the young men are circumcised at a river by an *ingcibi*, a specialist who performs the operation with a sharp spear. The young men are then draped in a blanket and painted with white clay. This shows that they are being cleansed in order to move into a different stage of their life.

The *abakhwetha*, or initiates, spend two to three months secluded in their hut. Their instructor, the *ikhankhatha*, teaches them the responsibilities of manhood and the proper respect for their cultural heritage. They learn the *hlonipa* language, in which special words of respect are substituted for particular names and terms. They also learn praise songs about themselves and their families.

After the period of seclusion, the young men step out of the hut. The hut and its contents are set on fire, and the young men run away without looking back. This symbolizes that they have turned their backs on their childhood. They are then washed, smeared with red ocher, given new clothes, and brought back to the community as *amakrwala*, which means young men. A goat is sacrificed to welcome them home.

Health authorities in South Africa now encourage Xhosa boys to take antibiotics before the ceremony and insist that the *ingcibi* sterilize the spear after each circumcision to prevent the spread of AIDS and other diseases.

In urban settings, these Xhosa customs are often adapted. Instead of thatch grass, which does not grow in the cities, the community may build an initiation hut that is covered with plastic.

Young rural women sometimes still undergo initiation when they reach puberty. This ceremony is known as *intonjane*. Unlike male initiation, which has survived in the urban areas, *intonjane* has been largely replaced in cities with the Western custom of celebrating adulthood at the twenty-first birthday party.

The one occasion on which the *abakhwetha* (male initiates) appear in public is to perform a dramatic dance. For this event, called *ukutshila*, they wear skirts and masks made of palm leaves.

Intonjane involves instruction about customs, adult roles, and *hlonipa* language terms. As with the men, initiates are taught in seclusion and colored with a white substance. Sacrifices are made to the ancestors.

▼ MARRIAGE ▼

Traditionally, marriage involved a process known as *ukuthwala*. This meant that the young woman was "kidnapped" by the prospective bridegroom with the help of his friends. The families then negotiated the *lobola* (bride-price) that her family had to be paid. Today *ukuthwala* takes place after the two families have already agreed to the marriage and to the *lobola*. This is seldom more than eight head of cattle, unless the woman is from a wealthy family.

Today Xhosa people generally have a Christian wedding ceremony, followed by a traditional ceremony that includes *lobola* negotiations. A family living in an urban area may decide that the *lobala* be paid in cash rather than in cows. Marriage is therefore an expensive event for most Xhosa men.▲

4

HISTORY

▼ EARLY CHIEFS ▼

Tshawe is revered as the first Xhosa chief. His name is so closely associated with royalty that, even today, Xhosa speakers still refer to the British royal family as amaTshawe. The story of Tshawe cannot be dated. The first Xhosa chiefdom dates back to 1736, by which time Phalo was ruling the Xhosa. His reign lasted from 1715 until 1775.

Phalo had two sons: Gcaleka, his heir, and Rharhabe. Rharhabe started Xhosa expansion west of the Kei River into the territory occupied by the Khoekhoe and the San. In the late 1700s, white colonists began to move into this area from the opposite direction. The great conflicts that resulted are part of the detailed records of colonial history.

We know far less about Xhosa chiefdoms located further east at this time. We do know that in the early 1800s, the paramount chief of the Thembu was called Ngubengcuku, or Vusani;

In the early 1800s the paramount chief of the Xhosa was a descendant of Gcaleka named Hintsa (above).

Gambushe ruled the Bomvana; and Faku ruled the Mpondo.

▼ TROUBLE IN THE WEST ▼

In the 1800s, the paramount chief of all the Xhosa was Hintsa, a descendant of Gcaleka. At this time, the junior Rharhabe branch was ruled by Ngqika. Until Ngqika came of age, his uncle Ndlambe acted as regent, or temporary ruler.

When Ngqika reached maturity, Ndlambe did not want to give up power. In 1800 he moved westward over the Fish River with many followers. There they settled in the territory that white colonists called the Zuurveld. This move split the Rharhabe into two. From then on they were called after their chiefs: the Ngqika and the Ndlambe. Other minor chiefs in the Zuurveld allied themselves with Ndlambe.

Competition for grazing land and cattle raids between white colonists and the Xhosa in the

Zuurveld had already caused three minor frontier wars. In the Fourth Frontier War (1811)
the British managed to push the Xhosa in the
Zuurveld east over the Fish River. Ngqika, in a
bid to increase his power, helped the British by
controlling Xhosa raids and territorial expansion. However, Ngqika's ambition lost him the
respect of Hintsa and increasingly eroded the
respect of his own following.

In 1818 Ngqika was defeated by Ndlambe,
who was assisted by the Gcaleka and others. A
diviner called Nxele played a leading role in
uniting the allies against Ngqika. He declared
that the God of the whites had punished whites
for the death of Christ by removing them from
their own lands. As a result they were now mov-
ing into Xhosa territory. But, he prophesied, the
Supreme Being of the Xhosa was stronger than
the Christian God and would help the Xhosa to
conquer the British and their ally, Ngqika.

After his defeat in November 1818, Ngqika
appealed for British assistance against Ndlambe.
This led to the Fifth Frontier War. The British
seized 23,000 cattle from Ngqika's enemies.
In return, Nxele led an invasion of the Cape
Colony and attacked Grahamstown in 1819.
Nxele was captured and sent to Robben Island.
He drowned while trying to escape from the
prison. The British helped Ngqika in the war. In
return for this favor, they forced Ngqika to leave

TROUBLE IN THE EAST

In 1819 Shaka, the powerful Zulu chief, had conquered most of the northeast coast of South Africa. People he defeated fled in all directions, raiding those they found in their path. The Hlubi, Bhaca, and Bhele were soon embroiled in this violent process.

The northernmost Xhosa chiefdom, the Mpondo ruled by Paramount Chief Faku, managed to fight off these attacks and to stay on Shaka's good side. The Bhaca were defeated by the Thembu and their Xhosa allies. They went on to defeat the Bhele and the Hlubi, and later returned to achieve victory against the Thembu. One of Shaka's most fearsome enemies was Mathiwane of the Ngwane, who harassed the Thembu, but was defeated by the British.

This terrible time of conflicts, known as the Mfecane, outlived Shaka, who had set it in motion. In 1828 Shaka and Ndlambe died; Ngqika died in 1829.

The Mfecane had brought new immigrants into the Eastern Cape. The Bhaca settled in the northern regions. The Hlubi, Bhele, and Zizi became poor refugees among the Gcaleka and the Thembu, who called them Mfengu, meaning hungry people in search of work.

his own territory between the Fish and the Keiskamma rivers. This region, known as the Ceded Territory, was the cause of further conflict.

In the decades that followed, the British continued to take over Xhosa land. Their aim was to push the Xhosa eastward and give the land to white settlers. Achieving this aim took a long time because the Xhosa resisted fiercely, and Britain had other wars to fight elsewhere.

▼ THE SIXTH FRONTIER WAR (1834–1835) ▼

An acute land shortage followed Ngqika's defeat in 1819. The Xhosa continued to graze their cattle in the Ceded Territory. A British patrol shot at a party of trespassing Xhosa who were grazing their cattle there. They wounded Ngqika's son, Xhoxho. This incident enraged the Xhosa. Their many grievances finally erupted into the full-scale Sixth Frontier War.

After nine months of war, Paramount Chief Hintsa was lured to British headquarters for talks. Although he had not played a direct role in the war, and the British had guaranteed Hintsa's personal safety, they held Hintsa hostage. The British demanded that the Xhosa pay 50,000 cattle and 1,000 horses as a fine.

Although the Gcaleka paramounts were highly respected by other chiefs, they did not have the direct authority over other chiefs to

The shooting of Paramount Chief Hintsa and the mutilation of his body caused international outrage. This illustration shows Harry Smith capturing Hintsa during the alleged escape attempt.

force such payment. Instead Hintsa was forced to join Colonel Harry Smith on an expedition to seize cattle, during which Hintsa was shot, and his body was terribly mutilated. Smith reported that Hintsa had tried to escape. An investigation of his death followed, but it did not remove the perception that Hintsa had been deliberately tricked and perhaps even murdered. This incident inflamed Xhosa hatred of the British.

As on previous occasions, the British now claimed as their victory prize all the land up to the Kei, the next river on their path to the east. They forced the Gcaleka over the Kei, and claimed the land between the Kei and the Keiskamma as a new British territory: the Province of Queen Adelaide.

The Mfengu had settled among the Gcaleka
as servants. Now they were "liberated" from the
Gcaleka by the British and allowed to settle in
the new province. Missionaries among the
Mfengu had turned them against the Gcaleka,
even though the Gcaleka had given the Mfengu
refuge when they fled from Shaka. The depar-
ture of the Mfengu created a lasting bitterness
against missionaries among the Gcaleka.

The Province of Queen Adelaide was later
dissolved by a liberal white governor, Andries
Stockenstrom. He also made treaties with Xhosa
chiefs. The treaties restored much of their
authority and permitted them to graze their
cattle in land that had formerly been off-limits.

▼ THE SEVENTH FRONTIER WAR
(1846–1848) ▼

When Stockenstrom was no longer governor,
his successors gradually removed the protections
that had been given to Xhosa chiefs. Tensions
grew until the Seventh Frontier War broke out in
April 1846.

Ngqika's son Sandile, like Hintsa, was imprisoned during negotiations with the British. Sir
Harry Smith, now honored with knighthood for
his achievements, forced Sandile to kiss his boot.
On another occasion he placed his boot on the
neck of Sandile's brother. Such disrespect only
heightened Xhosa hatred of the British.

To make peace, the Xhosa were forced to give up the former Province of Queen Adelaide. Smith renamed it British Kaffraria and made it part of the Cape Colony. He then divided it up into territories that he named after counties in Britain and even named chiefs' kraals after English cities: Sandile's kraal was named York. All Xhosa chiefs west of the Kei lost their independence. The British built several forts. They allowed many more Mfengu, who had fought on their side in the war, to settle in British Kaffraria.

During the frontier wars, many Xhosa houses were burned, crops were destroyed, and cattle were killed or stolen. The Xhosa who survived the frontier wars were utterly ruined. Many were forced to seek work in the Cape Colony. In the view of the historian Jeff Peires, "For the Xhosa, British Kaffraria was a monster which swallowed them up, tore them from their children, and squeezed them off their land onto the labor market."

▼ THE EIGHTH FRONTIER WAR
(1850–1853) ▼

A few years later, another diviner, named Mlanjeni, fanned Xhosa hopes of ridding themselves of the colonists. Once again, tensions began to mount. The British soon recognized that Mlanjeni was a threat.

Meanwhile, Smith meddled in Xhosa politics.

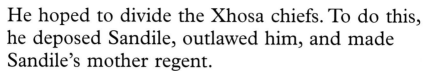

He hoped to divide the Xhosa chiefs. To do this, he deposed Sandile, outlawed him, and made Sandile's mother regent.

Before Mlanjeni could be captured, the Ngqika attacked. They burned colonial settlements and attacked the British forts. Gcaleka Paramount Chief Sarhili allowed his land to be used to hold captured cattle. The war was fought mainly by the Ngqika, Ndlambe, and Thembu. The Mfengu and Gqunukwebe, a Xhosa clan with Khoekhoe roots, fought on the side of the British.

As was usual procedure, the British burned Xhosa crops, and hunger forced the Xhosa to the negotiating table in 1852. The Ngqika refused to give up their ancestral land in the Amatola Mountains, but they agreed to a treaty that surrendered some Ngqika and Thembu land to the British.

▼ THE CATTLE KILLING ▼

In 1854 Sir George Grey became governor of the Cape Colony. He promoted the building of schools, roads, and medical facilities, and began farming, irrigation, and other projects to win the Xhosa over. Grey believed that such measures would convince the Xhosa to become "civilized." In the British view, that meant becoming more like the British.

Grey also changed the justice system and re-duced the power of the chiefs. Instead of chiefs

serving as judges for the clans in their regions
and fining offenders, British authorities took over
this function and paid the chiefs a salary. At the
village level, headmen were appointed to serve as
judges and report to magistrates. These measures
created a strict form of British control that
greatly reduced the authority of chiefs.

By the 1850s the Xhosa peoples closest to the
expanding Cape Colony had suffered great hard-
ships at the hands of the British Empire. Their
society had been radically altered. Paramount
Chief Sarhili of the Gcaleka, the most senior of
the Xhosa paramounts, wanted nothing to do
with the colonists or the missionaries and their
ideas about civilizing his people. For example,
he did not allow his people to wear Western
clothes because he regarded them as unclean.
He preferred the Xhosa custom of bathing daily
and anointing the body with a fresh coat of red
ocher.

At the beginning of 1855, lung sickness
spread eastward through the cattle herds in
British Kaffraria and across the Kei into Gcaleka
territory. The epidemic, introduced by European
cattle, killed more than 5,000 cattle a month. In
the words of a Xhosa saying, "Cattle are the
nation; if they are dead the nation dies." This
disastrous loss of cattle led many Xhosa to go
along with Grey's labor projects and his plan of
salaried chiefs. For many Xhosa it seemed that

only a miracle could now save their culture and society.

At this time, the British were involved in the Crimean War (1853–1856), where they were fighting the Russians. The Xhosa heard of this war and some began to identify closely with the Russians, since they shared the same enemy. They thought that the Russians must be black people like themselves and even perhaps the ancestors of the Xhosa. Some Xhosa hoped the Russians would sail to South Africa and help them fight the British.

A Xhosa man called Mhalakaza was a diviner and former Christian. Around March of 1856 he sent his young niece, Nongqawuse, and a companion called Nombanda to chase the birds from the fields. They went down to a river for a break. There they experienced a supernatural vision. Two ancestral spirits appeared to them and gave them a message. They said that the ancestors of the Xhosa would all soon return to earth and drive the whites and their allies into the sea. To prepare for this, the Xhosa people had to kill all their cattle, scatter all their stored grain, and stop farming. Then, the spirits instructed, new kraals and grain bins had to be built to hold the huge increase in grain and cattle that would follow.

Other prophets had urged similar actions before. But this prophesy found many believers.

Nongqawuse's prophesies led the Xhosa to kill their cattle and destroy their crops in the hope that their ancestors would free them from the whites and bring them greater wealth. In fact the cattle killing destroyed the power of the Xhosa, as the song below recalls. This photograph of Nongqawuse (right), was probably taken in 1858, after the cattle killing.

THE NONGQAWUSE SONG

Hayi uNongqawuse	Oh! Nongqawuse!
Intombi kaMhlakaza	The girl of Mhlakaza
Wasibulala isizwe sethu	She killed our nation
Yaxelela abantu yathi kubo bonke	She told the people, she told them all
Baya kuvuka abantu basemangcwabeni	That the dead would rise from their graves
Bazisa uvuyo kunye ubutyebi	Bringing joy and bringing wealth
Kanti uthetha ubuxoki	But she was telling a lie.

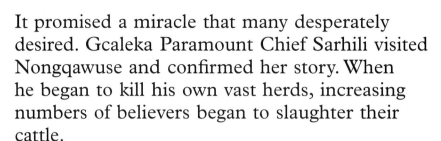

It promised a miracle that many desperately desired. Gcaleka Paramount Chief Sarhili visited Nongqawuse and confirmed her story. When he began to kill his own vast herds, increasing numbers of believers began to slaughter their cattle.

But there were nonbelievers too. The prophesy threw into conflict the two values that the Xhosa held most dear: their ancestors and their cattle. However, that combination led many others to regard the prophesy as logical and true. That is because Xhosa religion is based on the under-standing that ancestors only bring benefits to their relatives if they are honored with cattle sacrifices.

By February of 1857 there was widespread famine. At least 15,000 Xhosa people starved to death in British Kaffraria. East of the Kei River, among the Gcaleka and Thembu, at least 40,000 died. The power of the Xhosa chiefs was destroyed.

Grey refused to offer any relief against the starvation. He realized the famine would finally drive the Xhosa off their land and force them to become workers for the colonists. The popula-tion of British Kaffraria dropped from 105,000 to 37,700. In 1857 impoverished Xhosa num-bering 29,000 were sent to the Cape Colony as laborers. It is estimated that 150,000 Xhosa were displaced by the end of 1858. Colonists moved in and occupied the empty land.

This drawing shows the Xhosa chiefs imprisoned on Robben Island after the cattle killing. Many other political prisoners have been held here, including Nelson Mandela. In the background, the flat-topped Table Mountain can be seen behind the city of Cape Town.

▼ THE LAST FRONTIER WAR (1877–1878) ▼

In 1858 Grey sent troops against Sarhili, hoping to open Gcalekaland up to white settlement. The Gcaleka fled over the Mbashe River, and the British claimed their land. The Gcaleka were outraged when the British gave half of the vacated Gcaleka territory to their old enemies, the Mfengu, whom they soon attacked. The British became involved, and this led to the Ninth Frontier War.

Some chiefs made a last attempt to resist the British; others sided with the British. The Ngqika finally lost their territory west of the Kei, and Gcalekaland was conquered. One by one each of the paramount chiefs' territories fell under British control. The last territory to be taken over by the British was Mpondoland in 1894.▲

chapter

5

ARTS AND LITERATURE

▼ XHOSA BEADWORK ▼

In many African societies, elaborate beadwork is worn only by kings and diviners. Xhosa society, unlike the others, has permitted all members to wear beadwork during the last hundred years. Xhosa beadwork is among the finest made in Africa.

In rural communities, certain types of beadwork are worn by particular age groups and sexes. By looking at beadwork worn on ceremonial occassions, it is possible to tell somebody's marital status and seniority.

In the same way that traditions such as circumcision have been adapted to contemporary circumstances, so too has Xhosa beadwork. It has been used to convey a range of meanings at different times.

Nelson Mandela wore his full beaded Thembu outfit for his court sentencing in 1962. This was

Xhosa beadwork was made by women both for their own use and as gifts for men. The long strips seen here are anklets. The other items were stitched onto men's tobacco bags.

a sign of his pride in his own culture and his rejection of the apartheid justice system.

Later, beadwork began to be viewed negatively by many black South Africans. This was because homeland leaders, whom many regarded as puppets of the apartheid government, encouraged tradition as a way of increasing their power. Beadwork and other traditions declined in popularity because many people did not want to be associated with homeland leaders and conservative politics. Also beadwork became too expensive for many people.

However, diviners continued to wear their special beaded outfits, composed largely of white beads. White symbolizes purity and the special

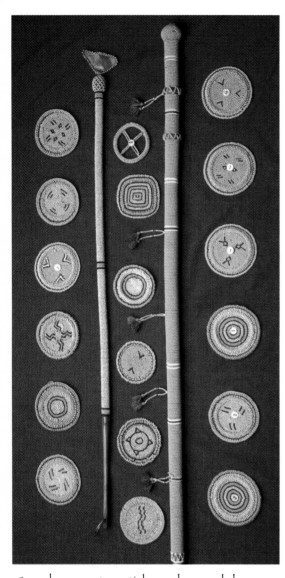

Seen here are two sticks and several decorations for tobacco bags. All are made with pink and blue beads, which were fashionable colors in Xhosa beadwork in the mid-1990s.

connection that diviners have with the spirit world. Some Xhosa women proved that beadwork did not have to be politically conservative. They created beaded flags in the colors of the ANC, showing their resistance against apartheid and homeland leaders.

Apartheid and homelands are now gone. Leaders in the new South Africa are once again proudly wearing beadwork and traditional dress as a sign of pride in their heritage. Nosimo Balindlela, current Minister of Education in the Eastern Cape, often appears on national television wearing her Xhosa costume.

This photograph shows a detail of the chest area of an outfit for special occasions. This kind of outfit was worn by senior Thembu men in the 1950s or 1960s. Numerous necklaces combine to make a powerful impression.

▼ ORAL LITERATURE ▼

Xhosa people had literature long before missionaries began to write and print the Xhosa language. There has always been oral literature—literature that is handed down from one generation to the next by word of mouth. Oral literature includes *iintsomi*, or folktales; *izaci namaqhalo*, sayings that communicate traditional wisdom, including idioms and proverbs; and i*zibongo*, or oral poetry.

▼ THE *IMBONGI* ▼

The key figure in Xhosa oral literature is the *imbongi* (plural: *iimbongi*), also called the praise singer or oral poet. Almost always men, *iimbongi* continue to play a vital role in society.

Traditionally, the *imbongi* lived close to the chief's great place and accompanied the chief on important occasions. Dressed in an animal skin hat and cloak, he carried a spear and a club called a knobkerrie. His public performances, which were sometimes prophetic, praised the chief's actions and best features. He also criticized the chief if aspects of his reign or government were unpopular.

The *imbongi* expressed his own poetic interpretation of events and also reflected what the people around him thought. He often conveyed his messages indirectly, using comparisons and metaphors. One way the *imbongi* emphasized his

POLITICAL CONFLICT AND THE *IIMBONGI*

During the apartheid regime, oral poets who criticized homeland leaders were sometimes silenced or banned. The former independent homeland of the Transkei provides an interesting example. As in most homelands, there was great conflict over whether or not to accept the idea of a homeland at all.

The rightful leader of the Thembu was Paramount Chief Sabata Dalindyebo, with whose family Nelson Mandela had grown up. Dalindyebo was against the idea of an independent homeland of Transkei. He supported the ANC, which fought for a unified South Africa without homelands. The apartheid government bypassed Dalindyebo and gave power to Chief Kaizer Matanzima, a lesser chief who later became Prime Minister of independent Transkei.

The conflict between these two chiefs came to a head in 1982 when Matanzima deposed Dalindyebo. The reason given was that he had criticized Matanzima and, in doing so, had broken the law.

Matanzima was angered by Dalindyebo's official praise singer, Melikhaya Mbutuma. In one poem, Mbutuma compared Matanzima to a water lizard and a skunk. The skunk is both black and white; the water lizard is at home both on land and in the water. The poet implied that Matanzima wanted the best of both worlds: black and white. The poet prophesied that this greed would result in people regarding Matanzima as rotten and stinking. Because of such critical poetry, Mbutuma was charged with inciting the people against Matanzima.

Paramount Chief Sabata Dalindyebo died in exile in Zambia. When his body was returned to Transkei, Matanzima had the corpse seized from the funeral parlor. He had it buried in a women's graveyard as a final insult. But when Matanzima was later overthrown, as the poet predicted, the paramount's body was reburied at Bumbane Great Place, his rightful resting place.

The well-known *imbongi*, Bongani Sitole, performed at the reburial ceremony of Paramount Chief Sabata Dalindyebo, whose remains were returned to the Transkei in 1989. Sitole wears the ANC colors on his cloak and his T-shirt, which also has the slogan "ANC LIVES."

words was by repetition. This form of poetry is often spontaneous, or made up on the spot. This also makes it unique.

The *imbongi* acted as a mediator, or go-between, among the chief and his people. Today political power has shifted away from the chiefs to new organizations and individuals, such as church groups, the ANC, and leaders like Mandela. Poets are praising these new powers together with, or instead of, traditional chiefs.

There are many oral poets today. Some dress in business suits; others decorate themselves in beadwork or animal skins. Today women and young people are also performing as *iimbongi*. Poems are produced not only in Xhosa, but also in English by poets such as Mzwakhe Mbuli, who performed at President Mandela's inauguration. Mzwakhe Mbuli combines Zulu praise poetry—similar to the Xhosa tradition—with contemporary music. His style reaches all the people of South Africa, and he is a very popular star.

▼ OTHER ARTS ▼

Xhosa books with a religious bent were published during the missionary period. Starting in the 1840s, Xhosa newspapers that published written poems were established. The first Xhosa novel was published in 1909 by S. E. K. Mqhayi, a respected figure in Xhosa literature. Later, several other writers emerged.

Traditional music and dance continue to be popular. They are celebrated at competitions and ceremonies. Popular music based on traditional forms is played by several groups, such as Amampondo.

THE XHOSA TODAY

The Xhosa people are an extremely powerful group within South Africa. They have made significant contributions to the creation of the new South Africa. They hold many powerful positions in government and in the ANC and other political parties. They also play an important role in the economy as workers; as businesspeople and directors of large companies; as doctors, lawyers, and other professionals; and as academics and researchers.

All South Africans are now faced with a great challenge. After years of apartheid and oppression, they must rebuild their country in a fair and democratic way. But there are severe problems to overcome. These include a history of inferior education, shortages of proper housing, unemployment, and crime. To succeed, it is necessary to cooperate. This strong sense of community is expressed in a Xhosa proverb that many believe sums up the world view of the Xhosa people: *Umntu ngumntu ngabantu*—A person is a person by virtue of other people.

Xhosa artists sell wood carvings and beadwork to tourists and also produce a wide variety of works for galleries in large cities. Such artists show that Xhosa heritage is an important resource that can always be drawn on in creative new ways.▲

Glossary

apartheid Government system based on controlling people by keeping them in separate racial groups.

dialect A variation of a commonly accepted language.

diviner One endowed with supernatural powers who can see future events and interpret dreams.

elite A group that is privileged because of rank, wealth, or education.

exile Forced exit from one's country for political reasons.

ikomkhulu Official homestead of the chief and his family.

imbongi Praise singer, or oral poet.

kraal Cattle corral.

lobola Bride-price; cattle or money paid to bride's family by that of the groom.

migrant worker Someone who works far away from his or her home.

polygyny Custom of having more than one wife at the same time.

tribute Payment made to a ruler to show respect or as the price of protection.

For Further Reading

Broster, Joan A. *Amagqirha: Religion, Magic and Medicine in Transkei.* Cape Town: Via Africa, [1981].

Elliot, A. *The Xhosa and Their Traditional Way of Life.* Cape Town: Struik, 1987.

Kaschula, R. H. "Mandela Comes Home: The Poets' Perspective" and "Preachers and Poets: A Gift from God (interview with Rev. L. W. Xozwa)" *Karring 6: Magazine for Language Teaching* (Winter 1993): pp 6–7, 8–10.

Mandela, N. *Long Walk to Freedom.* London: Abacus, 1995.

Omer-Cooper, J. D. *History of Southern Africa.* 2nd ed. Portsmouth, New Hampshire: Heinemann, 1994.

Challenging Reading

Bedford, Emma (ed). *Ezakwantu: Beadwork from the Eastern Cape.* Cape Town: South African National Gallery, 1993.

Mostert, N. *Frontiers.* New York: Alfred A. Knopf, 1992.

Peires, J. *The House of Phalo.* Johannesburg: Ravan Press, 1981.

Index

ABOUT THE AUTHOR

Dr. Russell H. Kaschula grew up in the Eastern Cape. He is a senior lecturer in the Department of African Languages and Literatures at the University of Cape Town and formerly taught at the universities of Rhodes, Transkei, and the Western Cape. He has published widely in his field and lectured in the United States, Europe, Swaziland, and Ghana. A registered advocate of the Supreme Court of South Africa, he was recently selected to represent South Africa in the Young African Leaders Project, hosted by the U.S. Government. His latest works include *Communicating Across Cultures in South Africa: Toward a Critical Language Awareness* and a short story entitled "The Forgiver" in *Marimba*.

PHOTO CREDITS

Cover, pp. 8, 17, 21, 24, 28, 34, 36 by A. Elliot © McGregor Museum, South Africa; pp. 13, 18, 27 bottom © Eric. L. Wheater; p. 15 © AP/Wide World; pp. 20, 22, 25, 29, 30, 32, 33 by Jean Morris © McGregor Museum, South Africa; p. 27 top by Michele and Tom Grimm © International Stock; pp. 39 and 51 courtesy of the South African Library; p. 43 Cape Archives; p. 49 Burton Album, Cory Library; pp. 53, 54, 55 by Ira Fox, courtesy of Gary van Wyk; p. 58 courtesy of Russell Kaschula.

CONSULTING EDITOR AND LAYOUT
Gary N. van Wyk, Ph.D.

SERIES DESIGN
Kim Sonsky